Holding the Pencil

Encourage your child to hold the pencil properly. The child should hold the pencil gently in between the thumb and the forefinger, about 1 or 2 cm above the tip.

The pencil should rest on the middle finger for proper support. This gentle grip allows the child to move the pencil easily for smooth writing movements.

Left hand

This book will help you to observe which hand the child favors. If your child is left-handed, tilt the page at a clockwise angle so that the top left corner is slightly higher than the right. Place the paper slightly to the left of the child's body to prevent smudging of letters.

Right hand

Keep your hand relaxed.

Bend your fingers, not your arm.

Don't press the pen too hard.

T0159065

Practice

The handwriting of your child will improve if you encourage them to practice their motor skills constantly. You can encourage them to write on the sand, color the alphabets or cut alphabets with safety scissors.

A

Alligator

Ant

Trace the Letter.

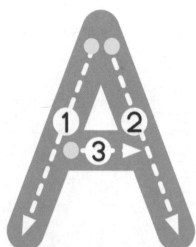

B

Bat

Bear

Trace the Letter.

C

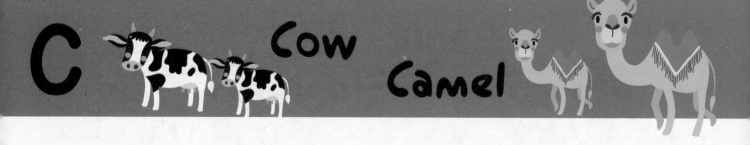

Cow

Camel

Trace the Letter.

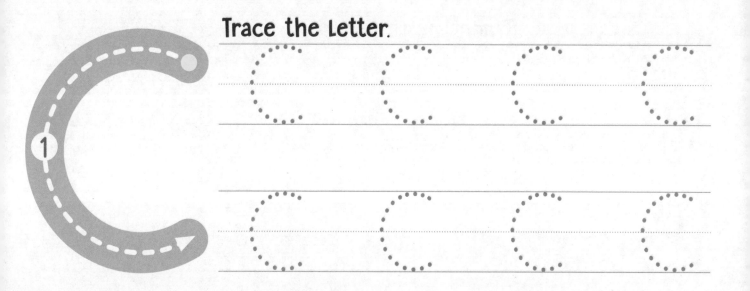

D

Duck

Deer

Trace the Letter.

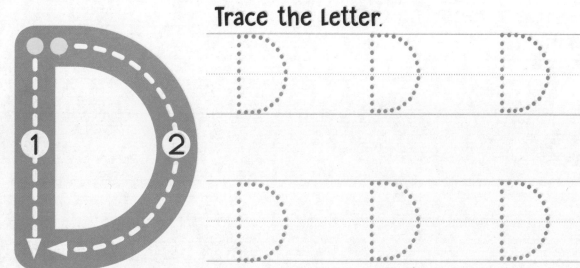

E

Eagle
Elephant

Trace the Letter.

E E E E

E E E E

F

Fish
Flamingo

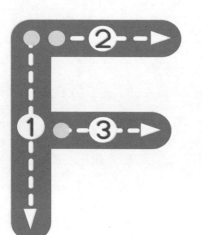

Trace the Letter.

F F F F

F F F F

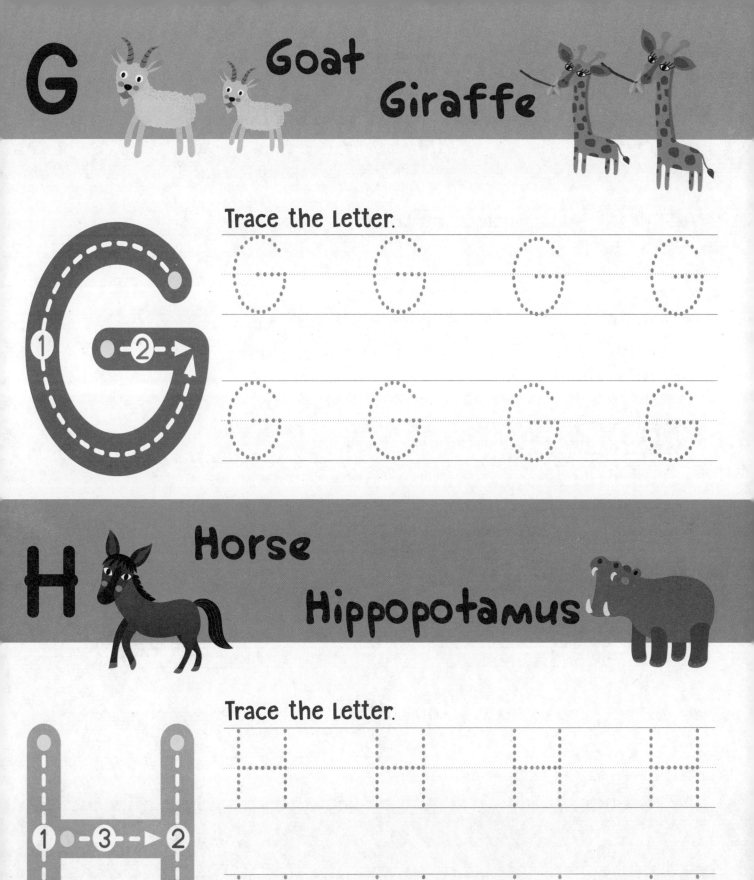

G

Goat

Giraffe

Trace the Letter.

H

Horse

Hippopotamus

Trace the Letter.

I

Insect

Iguana

Trace the Letter.

J

Jaguar

Jellyfish

Trace the Letter.

K

Kangaroo

Kiwi

Trace the Letter.

L

Lion

Lemur

Trace the Letter.

M

Mouse
Monkey

Trace the Letter.

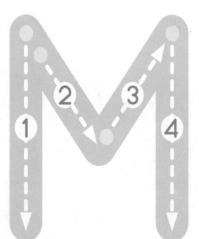

N

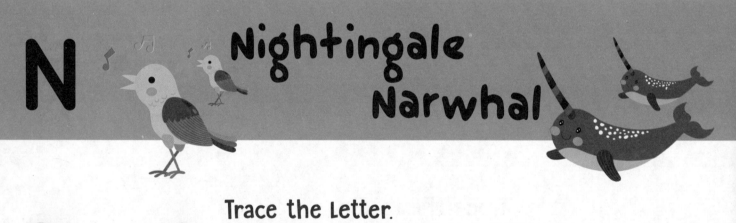

Nightingale
Narwhal

Trace the Letter.

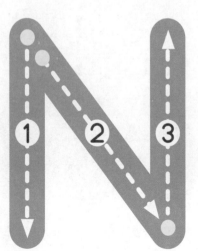

O

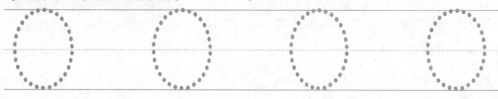
Orangutan

Owl

Trace the Letter.

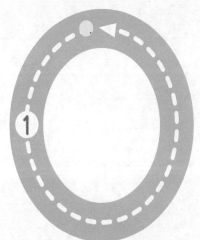

O O O O

O O O O

P

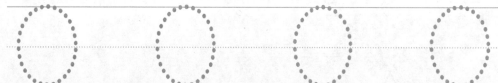
Penguin

Peacock

Trace the Letter.

P P P P

P P P P

Q

  Quail

Quokka

Trace the Letter.

Q Q Q Q

Q Q Q Q

R

 Rhinoceros

Rabbit

Trace the Letter.

R R R R

R R R R

S

Swan

Sheep

Trace the Letter.

S S S S

S S S S

T

Turkey

Tiger

Trace the Letter.

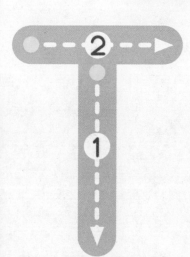

U

Urial
Umbrellabird

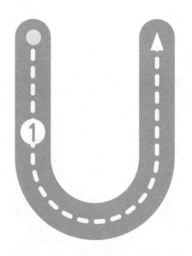
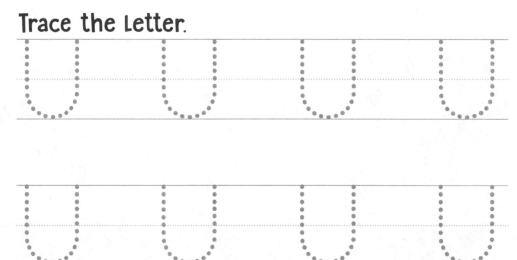

Trace the Letter.

V

Vampire Squid

Vulture

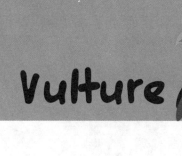
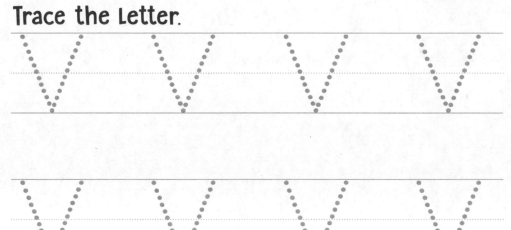

Trace the Letter.

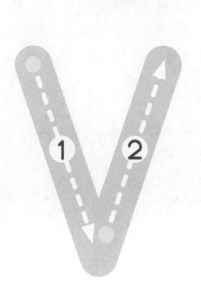

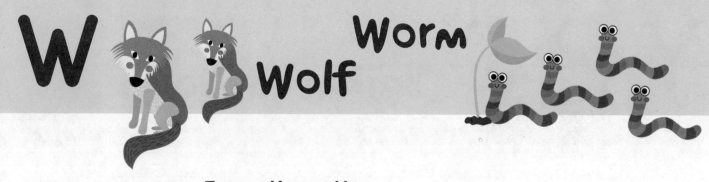

W

Worm

Wolf

Trace the Letter.

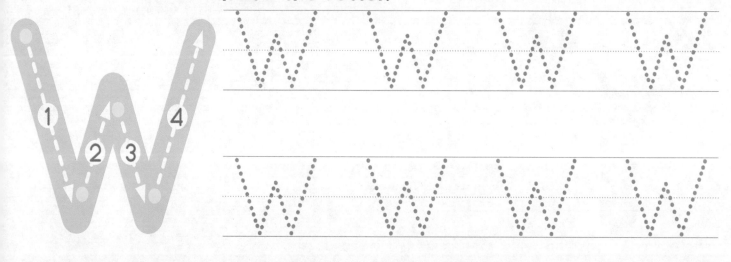

X

Xerus

X-ray Fish

Trace the Letter.

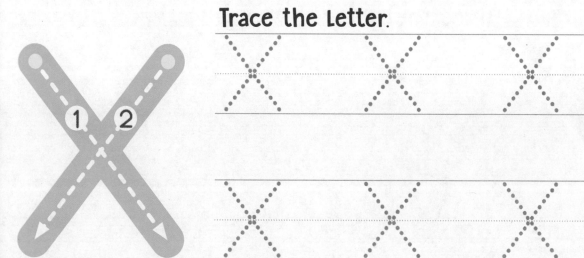

Y

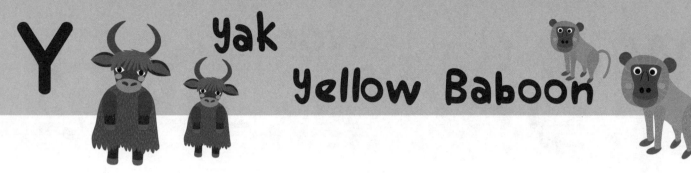

yak

Yellow Baboon

Trace the Letter.

Y Y Y Y

Y Y Y Y

Z

Zebra Finch

Zebra

Trace the Letter.

Z Z Z Z

Z Z Z Z

WRITE THE MISSING LETTERS.

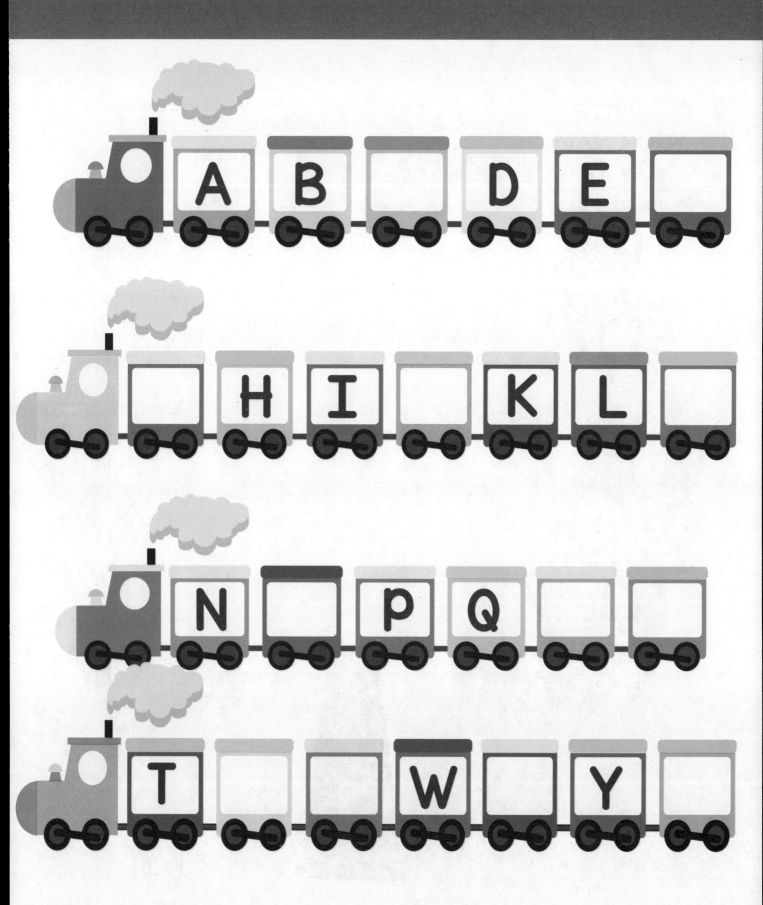

MY FAMILY TREE

WRITE THE NAMES OF YOUR FAMILY MEMBERS